Meelly
Finds a Family
And Everything Is Just Peachy

Mary T. Gavigan

BALBOA.
PRESS

A DIVISION OF HAY HOUSE

Balboa Press books may be ordered through booksellers or by contacting:

Balboa Press
A Division of Hay House
1663 Liberty Drive
Bloomington, IN 47403
www.balboapress.com
1 (877) 407-4847

Because of the dynamic nature of the Internet, any web addresses or links contained in this book may have changed since publication and may no longer be valid. The views expressed in this work are solely those of the author and do not necessarily reflect the views of the publisher, and the publisher hereby disclaims any responsibility for them.

The author of this book does not dispense medical advice or prescribe the use of any technique as a form of treatment for physical, emotional, or medical problems without the advice of a physician, either directly or indirectly. The intent of the author is only to offer information of a general nature to help you in your quest for emotional and spiritual well-being. In the event you use any of the information in this book for yourself, which is your constitutional right, the author and the publisher assume no responsibility for your actions.

Any people depicted in stock imagery provided by Thinkstock are models, and such images are being used for illustrative purposes only.
Certain stock imagery © Thinkstock.

Print information available on the last page.

ISBN: 978-1-4525-8571-0 (sc)
ISBN: 978-1-4525-8570-3 (e)

Library of Congress Control Number: 2013919580

Balboa Press rev. date: 10/16/2015

*In Loving Memory of my brother
Robert Anthony Gavigan who lost his
battle with cancer at the age of 49.*

V alentine's Day was just around the corner, and all of us were hoping to be picked to go to a new home. I had been here for only a couple of months, but others had been waiting for quite a while. My mom was living somewhere else, and I was hoping it would be my turn to leave next. I was a little scared because of the horror stories from those who had been returned. Still, I was hoping I would get a nice brother or sister.

One day, while I was just sitting and resting my eyes, a lovely couple approached me. The lady looked nice and said, "I think you would make Mary happy." *Yea!* I was so happy to finally be leaving the toy store! At the same time, though, I was sad. No more late nights playing with all the other bears once the storeowner left. *But it would be nice to have a sister.* I just hoped she wasn't one of those stuck-up girls I'd heard about who would tell me I was cute and then just leave me on the bed.

My new mom and dad gently put me in the car, and we drove for what seemed like forever. I was too short to see out the window, but I was so excited that I tried to stand up without them seeing me. But I was still too short. So I sat there and thought about all the possibilities ahead in a new life with my new sister.

Before too long, the car came to a stop. My mom and dad got out and gently picked me up. I looked around and saw a huge house—it was almost like a castle! I had never seen a house in real life; I'd only heard about them from bears that had been returned to the store. I thought to myself, *This place is huge! I sure hope my new sister is nice. I am going to do whatever I can to be nice to her.*

As I was carried through two big doors, all I could see were men and women walking around. My mom and dad stopped to talk to a few people. Everyone seemed to know each other and talked about someone named Mary. It made me wonder who Mary was. I also wondered who all these people were. Maybe they were relatives or workers. I really didn't know, but I was beginning to feel a little scared.

After a few more stops, we entered through another set of doors and walked toward a room. *Oh boy, this is it*, I thought. *I am going to finally meet my new sister!*

My mom held me behind her back as we walked into the room. I was so excited, but I couldn't see anything. *Please just give me to her*, I was thinking. *Hurry up!*

My mom and dad bent down, gave the girl named Mary a kiss, and said, "Look; we thought you might like some company." My mom held me out to Mary. She slowly sat up, put out a hand, and said, "Thank you. He is so cute."

I could not believe my eyes. I wasn't quite sure what this place was, but I didn't think it was their home. Big glass doors had cartoon characters on one side, and I spied a couch in the corner. This large room was filled with strange equipment. It was nothing like the kids' rooms I'd seen on TV. Then I remembered seeing places on TV where people go when someone is sick. This looked much more like that. *Maybe my new sister is sick*, I thought.

Mary hugged me and looked at me with a cute little smile even though her eyes were sad. From that moment, I knew I would be the best brother bear I possibly could be.

Mom and dad sat down on the couch and talked to Mary for a while. The whole time, Mary looked at me and rubbed my fur. It felt so good; her hands were warm on my back, and she tickled my feet. Nobody had rubbed me since my mother bear. I had almost forgotten how it felt.

Looking at me, she kept rubbing me and said that I was soft. It was hard for her to rub me because she had wires and tubes connected to one arm, but nonetheless, she kept petting me.

When mom and dad asked Mary how she was feeling, she gave a little smile and replied, "Just peachy." That was a saying I would come to love and even know when she was about to say it. Grownups kept talking to Mary about medical stuff. I really didn't know what they were talking about since I only knew some things from TV.

Suddenly, Mary blurted, "What should I name him? He has to have a name." She looked at me and so did my mom and dad. "I know, Meelly!"

My mom looked at her and said, "Meelly is a terrific name!" And so there it was—my name was Meelly.

Meelly, I thought. *I've never had a name before. Now I have a sister and a name! Oh, lucky me!*

Even though mom and dad were talking to Mary, she only looked at me. Smiling, she said, "Yeah, I like that name. Meelly. It's just you and me, Meelly." I was so happy. Mary seemed so nice and caring. I just hoped it stayed that way.

After a while, a couple of tall men came into the room. They started talking to Mary and my mom and dad about something called "surgery." I really had no idea what it meant. They were saying so many different things that I just could not keep up. Instead, I concentrated on Mary the whole time. I lay on the weird-looking bed while she rubbed my head and chubby tummy. I had to try hard not to laugh because sometimes it tickled. That was one thing my mom bear always told me: "Never let a human hear you."

Before too long, the men left. They had seemed nice, thoughtful, and caring. My mom called them "doctors." I also heard the word *surgery* again. This time, I thought I'd better listen and try to understand what they were talking about. Mom explained that in a couple of days Mary would have a biopsy. She told Mary not to worry and added, "The doctors just need to take a look at something in your body to try to make you better." mom also mentioned that it might hurt afterward, but this biopsy was very important.

The whole time my mom was talking, my dad just kept looking at my sister with sad eyes. Then smiling from ear to ear, he said, in his deep voice, "Everything is going to be all right. Don't you worry."

Mary said, "Okay," as though it was nothing really. Oops! There went my tummy again! Mary knew the perfect tickle spot.

Later that evening, Mary and I were finally alone. She looked at me and said, "Hmm, you are cute. It seems like it is just you and me now, Meelly. My parents went out for a while, and mom said she would be back later." With a tear in her eye, she added, "Well, I guess there is nothing I can do about this. I always knew this day would come, and so here it is."

Mary sighed and turned on the TV. She petted me the entire time I sat next to her. I couldn't help but think, *If she keeps this up, I won't have any fur left. Whoever heard of a bear without any fur? I've never seen a bald bear!*

Oh, well. I knew it was making my sister happy, which was all that mattered.

I felt sorry for Mary; she was so lonely and sick. Every time she tried to lie down on her back, she coughed and had to sit up. She tried placing pillows behind her neck to prop herself up and then a blanket, but nothing helped. Some ladies checked on her throughout the night. They put something in her mouth and asked if she was okay or needed anything. With a smile on her face, Mary answered, "Just peachy."

I knew she was getting tired, and I wondered how she was going to sleep since she kept coughing when she lay down. Finally, she lay on her side with me by her right arm.

Mary finally fell asleep for a while. I heard grown-ups and children talking in the hallway. *"From living in the toy store, I knew I could learn by looking around and listening to others"*. It was a noisy place. I couldn't figure out how sis could sleep through it; I like it nice and quiet when I am sleeping.

Sis was still sleeping when a lady came in and put a big tray on the table. It smelled like food, but sis just kept sleeping.

After what seemed like forever, my mom came in with a bag of food. *Wow, more food!* I thought. *This place can't be that bad. Look at all the food they give you!*

Mary woke and slowly sat up after mom kissed her on the forehead. "Now come on, you need to eat," mom urged. "I knew you wouldn't want to eat this hospital food, so I went out and got you something special." Mary really wasn't hungry, but mom insisted and said, "You need your strength for when you have surgery in a couple of days."

Sis sat up, put me by her pillow, and said, "Meelly, you can stay here while I eat."

When it was getting dark, mom reminded sis, "You need to get some rest because there will be a lot of tests the day before the surgery."

Picking me up, sis got comfortable on her side and gently placed me by her head. She softly said, "Good night, Meelly. Good night, mom." Closing her eyes, she went to sleep while mom stroked her hair.

I remained very still for two reasons. First, I really did not want to wake Mary up because she looked so tired. The second reason was that tears ran down mom's face while she was still rubbing Mary's hair. I knew this was not good. Once Mary was fast asleep, mom moved over to the couch and began reading a book. But once again, her eyes filled with tears. I was scared, but Mary, mom, and dad were scared too. I did the only thing I could think to do. I closed my eyes and went to sleep.

Sis must have been really tired. All night long, the lady in the white outfit kept coming in and putting something in sis's mouth and around her arm, but sis went right back to sleep each time. Little did I know this was something they do to all people who are sick. It helps the doctors learn more about the person's body and how to help him or her. I also learned that the people who kept coming in were called nurses. I overheard one of the ladies call the other lady "nurse." I guess that is her name.

I was used to getting up early at the toy store because it was one of the few chances we could play with each other. That morning, I woke up just as the sun was coming up. Sis was still sleeping while mom was cuddled up on the couch. I guess she must have slept there all night. *I wonder where dad is?*

Sis and mom did not get to sleep much longer. Doctors and nurses came in and explained that they needed to run a few routine tests before the surgery. Before I knew it, people were poking my poor sister with needles and using a big machine. I later heard it was called an X-ray machine and it took pictures of her bones! *I wonder if I have bones?* They have a portable X ray machine that goes into your room and they also have one in a special room. Everyone was talking to sis and mom about what would happen the following day. Mary just sat there while rubbing my tummy, nodding her head, and saying, "Okay," several times.

After all the people left, dad showed up. It was still early, but he had come to visit with his "special girl." mom and dad talked for a while, and I saw tears in their eyes. They were scared, but sis looked at them and said, "Now, mom and dad, everything is going to be fine. You both just take care of Meelly while I am in surgery and don't worry about me."

On the morning of the surgery, I knew Mary was scared even though she did not want to show it. She was trying so hard to be brave; mom and dad were scared too. What could I—little helpless Meelly—possibly do? Nothing. I couldn't talk to anyone. Even though I really did not understand what was truly going on, I was scared too.

Two men came and took Mary away in her bed. As they were leaving the room, she handed me to mom and said, "Don't forget to take care of Meelly. I'll be back later. I love you, mom and dad."

The hours seemed like days. Mom put me down on the couch before she and dad walked out of the room. Suddenly, I was alone and scared. Still, all I could think about was my sis and how she must have been feeling. I couldn't wait to see her. Impatient, I sat still as I watched and listened to all the people who walked by, hoping one of them was Mary. Finally, mom and dad came in and so did Mary's bed. But where was Mary? I was too short to see up into the bed.

After what seemed like another day, I heard a voice. It was sis's voice, and I was so happy! *Come on, someone, pick me up! I want to see her; I want her to rub my tummy!* I wanted to say. But no one picked me up. I saw mom and dad lean over her bed and ask how she was. All I heard were the faint words, "I am just peachy."

I smiled to myself and thought, *Yep, that's my sis.* Before long, more doctors and nurses talked with mom and dad. I heard them say that everything went fine and that they got a nice biopsy. They also said that it would take a day or so to determine what type of cancer it was. *Cancer, what is cancer?* I wondered. It didn't sound good, but sis was okay and back in the room. The good news was that she could go home after a week or so.

Boy, oh boy, was I happy! I would have been even happier if someone had just picked me up so I could see her. Suddenly, I saw sis, who was moving slower than before, trying to sit up. Mom and dad gently helped her to sit up a little. I noticed a little tear as she smiled and told mom and dad, "Don't worry; I'm okay."

I thought all hope was lost at that point and that she had forgotten all about me. *Who was I anyway? Just some bear. Maybe I was hoping too much for a family.* Suddenly, Mary asked, "Where's Meelly?"

Laughing, mom reached over, picked me up, and said, "So, you do remember him."

Sis said, "Of course." Once again, I was back on her bed. This time, she had more tubes and looked so pale. It was so hard to keep from crying, but I had to be strong. I remembered what I had said when I first saw her. It made me more determined to be the best brother bear I could be.

As the day went on, she slept a lot. But she always kept me by her head—in a way she was using me as a pillow. I think she liked my chubby tummy. I tried not to move while mom stroked her hair and dad paced back and forth.

After a full day, the doctor came in and said he had some news for them. Mary sat up with mom, dad, and me by her side. We listened patiently to what to the doctor was saying.

He explained that the tumor was about the size of a large orange. Because it was close to Mary's heart, they did not get enough of the tumor in the biopsy to run all the tests they wanted. With a sad look on his face, the doctor said that they would have to operate again first thing the next morning to remove more of the tumor. We stared at him with concern.

The doctor then looked at the cut in Mary's chest, which was now stapled together like a piece of paper. He explained, "By going in through the same spot, she would not have another scar."

Poor Mary, mom, and dad. *Are all humans sick like this?* I wondered.

After the doctor left, Mary finally cried and asked, "Why me? Why can't they just fix me?" mom and dad told her to have faith and believe; everything would be fine. Mary looked at me and said, "Boy, it sure would be nice to be a bear right now." Tucking me in by her neck, she quickly fell asleep.

As the days went by, Mary was feeling and doing better after the second surgery. Little did I know that she still had a long road ahead of her. Once the results came in, we learned that she had Hodgkin's disease. We also learned that it is a type of cancer in the lymph nodes that can spread. The fear was that it had spread to other organs in her body. Surgery number three was ordered. This was called exploratory surgery. By entering through her stomach, the doctor could look at all the organs to see just where the cancer was. That helped the doctors to know which medicines to give her to make her better.

My family was getting a little more used to the hospital and the procedures even though none of us became used to them entirely. Mary was a real trooper. Every time someone would ask her how she was, Mary's answer was always the same: "Just peachy." And I was right next to her all the time.

We became really close. She talked to me when no one was around, and I just looked at her and listened. I liked to think that she knew I could understand her. Over and over I thought, *I love my sister with all my little bear heart.*

The dreadful day came when the fourth surgery was scheduled. After kissing mom, dad, and me, Mary was wheeled off to surgery. This time, though, she came back very soon because of a problem just before the surgeon was to operate. Remember I told you that if she lay on her back she coughed? Well, the doctor said that the tumor over her left lung had become larger. With too much pressure on her left lung it made her left lung collapse prior to her surgery, which meant they had to cancel the surgery or she would have died.

When I heard that, all I could think about was mom and dad—how sad we all would have been if the surgery had taken place. I wished I could have stood up on my little, short legs and find the doctor who stopped the surgery. I wanted to give him a big hug and kiss for not letting my sis die. I never knew I could feel what was going on in my mind and heart. It was as though I were almost a real brother, not just a brother bear but also a human. *Could that be possible? Did I have human feelings?* Whatever I was feeling, I knew mom and dad felt it even more. I could see the love on their faces for their only daughter. How terrible it would be if something were to happen to her!

Days later, Mary had to start chemotherapy. Because she was stage 4B, which I later learned was not good, the doctors decided they would keep her in the hospital for the first few treatments. Nurses came in and hooked sis up to several tubes and injected four different types of drugs.

At first, Mary said that she felt a burning in her arm as the nurses put in the medicine. It hurt a lot, but the nurses said that was normal and the pain would go away. I didn't understand why they had to hurt her to make her feel better.

Suddenly, Mary told mom and dad that she was going to vomit. I didn't know what that was, but it sounded yucky. Then it came; Mary threw up. I had never seen anything like that; bears don't do things like that. Oh no, it happened again and again! Mom got the nurse, who said it was a side effect of the medicine. Giving Mary ice chips to suck on, they explained that this should help keep fluids in her.

Poor Mary! She kept throwing up for nine or ten hours. She was so tired, and I could see in her eyes just how sad she felt. Mom and dad looked so worried. I was worried and scared too and didn't know what to do.

What could I do? I was just a brother bear, so I stayed by her and wished for her to be okay. Finally, she was sleeping and I stayed by her head. She looked so peaceful, and I was glad. Mom and dad fell asleep on the sofa. *It's over*, I thought. *The terrible treatment is over.*

I was wrong, though. It was not over. It was just the beginning of a year of treatment with terrible drugs that were supposed to help Mary. How could anybody go through this for a year?

One day, mom and dad came into our hospital room and told Mary that it was time for her to go home. She would finish her treatments, but she didn't have to stay in the hospital for them. Mary was so happy! It was time to go home, so I was happy too!

While everyone got everything together for the journey, I began to wonder if my sis would forget all about me when we got home. I remembered other bears from the store saying that sometimes their human brothers and sisters just forget them over time. I hoped that wouldn't happen to me. I loved my sister and my mom and dad. I wanted to be the best brother bear I could be!

Mary picked me up, and we were wheeled out in a chair to the car. As she slowly climbed in, I could see she was very tired. But she still had a smile on her face, feeling everything was just peachy.

Once we were settled in the car, dad started driving. After riding for a while, Mary told mom how she was doing. Mom kept saying how nice it was for Mary to be able to come home and that everything was going to be fine. Nodding her head, Mary said, "Don't worry, and don't be sad. I am just peachy."

We arrived home and went into a pretty room. The walls were pink, and the bed was much bigger than the one at the hospital. As I looked around the room, I noticed a lot of bears and dogs and other animals on her bed. *Oh no, here it comes*, I thought. *Will this be the horrible day that I get tossed on the bed and forgotten?* It made me so sad; I wanted to be special to Mary. I'm Meelly. I have a name, and I was there when she was sick. I listened to her talk when she was sad, and I am her brother bear. I am special.

Mom helped Mary into bed, covered her up, and told her to get some sleep. Meanwhile, I was sitting on a chair across the room where mom had put me. *Come on, get me! I am over here! Don't forget about me! Yoo-hoo, hello! Here I am, your pillow bear!*

What was I thinking? All the other bears and animals started laughing at me. One dog said, "What, do you think she can hear you? Remember, we can only talk to each other. Mary isn't going to play with you anymore. She goes to school and has human friends; she doesn't have time for us. Don't worry," the dog said. "You will get used to it. We will be your friends."

"No," I said. "I am Meelly. I am her brother bear. I want to make her happy." When I told them about the things that had gone on at the hospital, they were shocked. The dog with the long ears told me Mary had been coughing for a long time and that mom and dad kept taking her to the doctors. Then a white furry rabbit said Mary was always so tired and pale, and then one day they took her away and now she was back. All of the animals didn't really know what was going on, but mom and dad would come home sometimes and cry. They told me that they talked about her dying and how scared they were.

I told these animals that Mary wasn't going to die. They were giving her medicine. Even though it made her sick, the medicine would make her better. We looked at one another and then looked at Mary. She was so still. All of us thought she was sleeping, but she wasn't. She sat up and looked around. Mom was close by and asked what she wanted. Mary said, "I want Meelly. Where is he?"

What did I just hear? I said to myself.

All the animals looked at me. "What does she mean she wants you?" said the dog. "I have been here since she was a baby! Why does she want you?"

Mom picked me up and gently placed me by Mary's hand and said, "Here you go." sis looked at me, gave me a little kiss on my nose, and put me by her head. I was so happy and watched over her as she closed her eyes and fell asleep.

Our days were pretty simple. Dad would get up and go to work, and mom encouraged Mary to eat some breakfast even though she always said that she wasn't hungry. Mom reminded her she had to keep up her strength.

After a few weeks of chemotherapy, Mary was feeling a little better. She wanted to go to school even though she still had cancer. She told me that she missed her friends, but she didn't miss all the homework.

I had heard about school from listening to Mary and mom talk. Mary had really nice friends who had visited her at the hospital and her home but there where some girls who made fun of her when she lost part of her hair. I wanted to tell the girls to be nice but I couldn't and sis didn't want to tell mom because she didn't want mom and dad to worry more. Mary got so busy going to school when she could and getting her medicine every week. I had that heavy thought again. *Oh no, here it comes. Sis is going to forget about me since she is so busy.* Plus, the other bears and doggies in her room would make fun of me. Maybe I shouldn't have told them that she loved me and that I was her special brother bear.

One day, Mary said her head hurt. Mom gave her some medicine to make it stop hurting, but it only got worse. Mom always stayed in Mary's room to watch over her. Mary was quiet and did not complain much. She whispered to me that she felt bad for mom and dad and didn't want them to worry more than they already did. So every time someone would ask her how she was, she simply said, "Just peachy."

But something was wrong with my sis that day. Her head really hurt, and nothing mom did took the pain away. I felt so sad for Mary and didn't understand why the other animals didn't care. Maybe I was becoming more like a human; all I know is that I wanted to make my sis feel better. As she played in bed with me by her head, tears ran down her cheeks because she was in so much pain. I tried to understand the pain, but I'm just a bear and don't know what it feels like.

Mom asked Mary if she felt any better. Mary said she just needed some sleep and would feel better in the morning. Mom stayed with us, rubbing Mary's hair to help her fall asleep, but it wasn't working. I tried to stay still and not bother her, but it was hard. Her tears fell onto my fur, It was really dark out now, and sis was still in so much pain. I wanted to know what pain was, and then maybe I could do something to help her. Poor sis could not fall asleep and was crying. Mom wanted to take her to the hospital, but sis didn't want to go.

Mom insisted and helped Mary get dressed. I was so scared and didn't know what was going to happen, but I knew that I wanted to go with her. A bear named Stripes told me sis would come back, so I stayed in her bed. I watched sadly as mom, dad, and sis walked out of the room.

Suddenly, mom came back and picked me up. I was so happy sis didn't forget about me, but she didn't look happy. Sis was pale and could not walk very well. Mom helped her get in the car and put me next to her. Sis held on to me and tried not to cry. Dad drove very fast to the same place where they took me the first time. It was really dark out, but I knew it was the same place because it was so big. A few people came to help sis out of the car and put her in the funny-looking chair on wheels.

Mom picked me up and put me on Mary's lap. I was happy to be there, but I was also scared because I didn't know what was going to happen. All I knew was that I wanted sis to be okay. Mom and dad followed the people who were called nurses. The nurses helped the doctors make sis better.

They put sis in a bed; mom put me on a chair. I was so short that I couldn't see what they were doing. I wished my legs were long like Stripes's instead of my fat, little legs. So I just sat there waiting for Mary to ask for me. I don't remember how long it was before Mary finally asked, "Where is Meelly?"

Mom put me on Mary's tummy. All I could see were tubes that once again were connected to her. I felt sad. *But I can't feel things. I'm a bear,* I thought to myself. Mary took me and placed me by her head, as she always liked to do. Now I could finally hear what everyone was saying. I tried to listen and understand, but I didn't know what a lot of their words meant. I only knew simple words from listening to the TV and the other bears at the store, so I tried to really listen.

There was something wrong with Mary's blood. *Hmm, what is blood? I don't have blood.* I thought. But I knew something wasn't right. I listened and learned that humans have blood in their body. Sometimes, the blood can have an infection in it. Wow, *infection*—that's another new word I am learning. An infection is something that goes wrong in a human's body. Medicine helps the person to get better. Sis looked so tired; her eyes kept closing as if she wanted to sleep. She was given more medicine in the tubes, and she finally fell asleep. My poor sis was so sick. Once again, I knew I had to be the best brother bear to help her get better. While sis was sleeping, the doctor talked to mom and dad. If they hadn't brought sis to the hospital, she would have died by the next day. When I heard that, I almost moved because I knew what death was. Instead, I tried to be very still because they said she needed sleep and medicine to make her better.

After a few days with Mary sleeping a lot, she felt a little better. I was so happy. She started to talk to me again and rub my big belly. It tickled so much, especially when she rubbed behind my ears. All this time, the doctors and nurses checked on sis. Sometimes, mom slept on the couch just like the very first time they brought me here. I heard them talking and learned the chemotherapy was so strong that it made her blood bad. I was getting kind of smart because I was listening to everyone when they talked. It was almost as though I was human. I began to have feelings like humans do. Every once in a while, my face would get a little wet like my sis's. I later learned those were tears.

I don't know how long we stayed at the hospital, but it was days and days. They would not let sis go home until her blood was better. One day, the doctor came in with the news that we could go home. All of us were so happy. *Yea! Sis is all better, and no more hospital,* I kept saying to myself. *We can go home, and she can play with me! Everything will be fine.*

What I didn't know was that she still needed more of the chemotherapy medicine. But sis was happy, so I was happy. Sis had to stay at home and rest for a few weeks. That's when I found out that there are seven days in a week. I wasn't just getting feelings; I was getting smart too. Mary was the best sister I could ever ask for, and I wanted to be the best brother bear I could be. The other animals asked me what had happened, so I told them as much as I could remember. They were happy that sis was home again even though she didn't play with them as much as she played with me.

Every time mom or dad, and sometimes even sis's friends, took sis to get her chemotherapy, she would take me along. I was her little pillow by her head. I was special. I wasn't like the other animals.

One day when mom and dad took sis to get her chemotherapy, there was a problem. So I did what I did best, which was to listen. The veins in Mary's arms were not working well because the medicine burns them, which makes it harder for more medicine to go in. The doctor told mom, dad, and sis that they could put a tube in her chest and put the medicine in through the tube. Once again, I was confused, but I was getting use to that. I never knew before that humans were so different from us bears, but they are.

Mary agreed to the tube being put in her if it would help. I was proud of Mary for always doing whatever the doctors said without complaining— well, almost. I do remember a funny time when we went to chemotherapy. When the nurse tried to find a vein in Mary's foot, she kicked the nurse. It was so funny. I tried very hard not to laugh out loud so they wouldn't hear me.

Another surgery was planned. Mom and dad always seemed sad and worried. I was worried too, but I knew she would be okay. Mary always smiled and tried to make everyone feel good. She hardly ever complained and just watched TV or drew cartoon pictures. She liked to draw pictures of a dog named Snoopy resting on top of his dog house. It was nice to see her smile. Friends from school visited her at home and in the hospital and brought cards and flowers. Even though Mary was sick, she was still happy.

The big day came, and the doctors put a tube in her chest called a Hickman catheter. The long, white tube came out of her chest. The medicine would go in there instead of in her arms. Her arms were black and brown from the medicine that they put in her arms. The medicine burned her veins, and with no more veins they could use, the doctors said they had to do this. Sis simply said, "Okay."

It seemed weird that she never really complained. But I knew she was tired and sore because she talked to me when no one was there. She always told everyone else that she was, "Just peachy."

After the tube was in her chest, the doctors showed her how to clean it every day. What she had to do seemed kind of weird, but the doctors told her it would help her. Sis and mom decided that they should give the tube a name. That way, when she was at school, no one would know what they were talking about. So they named it Mikey. *What a silly name,* I thought. But they named me Meelly, so maybe they like those types of names. It didn't matter. I was her brother bear, so I was happy.

After sis had the Hickman put in, it was so much easier for her to get her chemotherapy. From that point on, we all got into a routine. When sis went in for her medicine, she always took me with her. I was so happy that she loved me and that I could help her by being her pillow or just someone to rub.

Actually, all that rubbing was really starting to show on me. One day, as sis held me in her arm, we walked by a mirror and I saw myself. *Oops ... where did my hair go?* I noticed my fur was all patted down. I looked a little squished too, but it was okay. If Mary could go through all this, a little less fur on me was just fine.

Finally, the day came that was to be her last treatment. Yea! No more hospitals. Sis was feeling better and looking forward to going back to school instead of going to the hospital. But we were wrong. The doctor walked into the hospital room and talked to sis and mom and dad. I was used to listening by now, so I just sat still and tried to understand what the doctor was saying.

He explained that Mary needed radiation therapy. *What? What is that?* I wondered. I hoped it was not as bad as the chemotherapy medicine because I did not like watching sis get so sick from the medicine.

The doctor explained that radiation treatment would kill any cancer that still might be in her body.

I heard the words, but I really didn't understand them. It was all so confusing. Bears don't get sick, but poor sis needed more treatment. The doctor also stated that she would need radiation for a few months. *Oh no,* I thought, *more throwing up.* I hoped there wouldn't be more throwing up because that was not a good thing.

Sis looked at mom, dad, and the doctor before saying, "When do we do this?" The doctor explained they had to make marks like little dots on her chest so they knew where to put the radiation. They wanted to radiate only the tumor, not her heart and lungs.

So sis returned to the hospital. Once again, she propped me up by her head. I was glad that she didn't forget about me. When the doctors came in and took Mary away, I stayed in the room with mom and dad. We waited together for Mary to be brought back. Poor mom and dad, they were so sad that their daughter was not better.

When sis was brought back to the room, she told us what they did. First, a doctor drew on her chest to mark which areas should be blocked from the radiation. Next, metal blocks were made to cover those areas when she was on the radiation table. This would prevent the radiation from hitting her heart and lungs too much.

Days later, sis had her first treatment. Mom, dad, and I waited for her in her room. Finally, after what seemed like hours, the nurses brought sis back. She looked okay and didn't throw up. But she did say that she was tired. The doctor had explained that radiation makes the patient very tired depending on how much was used. We knew the doctors gave her a lot to make the tumor go away.

Mom and dad asked her how she was, and once again she answered, "I'm just peachy." That was my sis. I loved her, and she loved me. No matter where we were, I was always next to her, and I was happy. Even though she was sick, she didn't forget about me, and I was glad to be her brother bear.

After being treated a few times by radiation, sis started to lose her hair from the middle part of the back of her head. It was really weird, but she was kind of like me now. I didn't have a lot of fur, and she didn't have a lot of hair. The difference was that nobody could tell she had lost some hair because the top of her hair was long enough to cover it up. Sometimes, she pulled her hair up and joked around that she was half-bald. Trying to make everyone happy, she was always laughing and joking around. But I knew that she was sad because she talked to me. After more treatments her skin started turning brown; Mary loved it. She had a nice tan without spending hours in the sun, which could cause skin cancer.

I was learning a lot by listening, but I hadn't heard about skin cancer before. One night, when sis was asleep, I heard mom and dad talking about the different cancers that a person can get. Dad mentioned that once you have cancer, you can get another type of cancer easier.

I was confused. How could someone get cancer again? Sis had a lot of medicine and still could get cancer again? I didn't understand, so I did what I did best and remained still to let sis sleep. I knew that when she woke up, she would rub my chubby tummy.

Finally, all the radiation was over. No more treatments! Mary was in something called remission. That means the cancer was not in her body anymore.

We were all so happy to hear the great news. Once again, Mary could be a normal girl. Then I got scared. *What if she forgets about me again?* I suddenly remembered what all the other bears and doggies at our house had said about Mary being too busy to play with them. Plus, sis was getting older. No one plays with bears when they are older. Even though I was sad, I was happy for sis and my mom and dad. Sis was all better now, which was the only thing that mattered.

Sis was able to return to school. I knew that mom and dad were still worried about her, but that is what moms and dads do. They worry about their children to make sure they are okay.

One day, while Mary was at school, mom was cleaning Mary's room. Mom put me on the chair with the other animals. My tummy felt funny, and my face got a little wet like that time when I was sad. The other animals laughed at me and said I was being silly, but I told them that they didn't understand. I was the one who had been there for sis the whole time she was sick. They didn't understand it too well because they didn't see her sick all the time. But I didn't care what they said; I was just happy that I was the best brother bear I could be.

Mary came home from school and went to her room to rest, as she still tired easily. I could hear the voice in my head say, *Hello, I am over here. Remember me? My name is Meelly.*

When mom came in to see how sis was doing, I heard sis say, "Where is Meelly? I want him on my bed."

Yea! That was my sis. She didn't forget about me. I had told the other animals that I was special just like my sis.

From that day on, sis always kept me on her bed. Sometimes, she still used me as a pillow as she had in the hospital.

I finally had my new home with my new family, and sis was all better, and everything was going to be great from then on. Sis still had to go the big hospital for checkups every few months to make sure the cancer hadn't come back. Fortunately, the tests were always good, and everyone was happy.

As the years went by, sis and I were always together. She took me with her whenever she spent the night somewhere else. We had a good life together. I was her brother bear, and she was my sis. I knew we would always be together no matter what the future brought. Years later, sis was not feeling good. *Oh no,* I thought as a tear fell from my eye.

Printed in the United States
By Bookmasters